200+ Fun & Funky Embroidery Designs

The dozens of original, transfer designs in this book are perfect for embellishing and personalizing your home and wardrobe with colorful embroidery. Embroidery is the wonderful take-it-along handwork you can pick up and put down whenever and wherever you want to create with needle, thread, and fabric—no messy supplies or special tools required. The beauty of it is you can enjoy this relaxing pastime whether you're travelling on a long trip, watching an evening of TV, or just waiting for the kids at the dentist.

Transfers are ready to iron onto everything from T-shirts and jeans to baby bibs and totes. It's that easy then you're all set to embroider. Each transfer can be used three or more times, offering plenty of options for repeating patterns and coordinating sets. Choose tropical motifs to embroider a summer outfit, complete with calypso pants, cotton shirt, and matching handbag for a set you'll love to show off. Accent your home with the elegance of embroidered bed linens and tea towels, or stitch a gift of sweet embroidered bibs for an upcoming baby shower. With something for every style and season, this book is sure to become a favorite resource for your embroidery projects as well as other arts and crafts, including appliqué, leatherwork, woodburning, and fabric painting.

Embroidery basics are easy to master and even a beginner will be stitching like a pro with the help of the stitch diagrams and instructions on page 6. Check out the project gallery on pages 43-48 for inspiration and ideas for choosing embroidery stitches. When shopping for supplies, be sure to ask about the fabulous embroidery threads now available on the market, including precious metals, jewels, antique pearlescent shades, fluorescent and glow in the dark tones. Embroidery has never been so much fun!

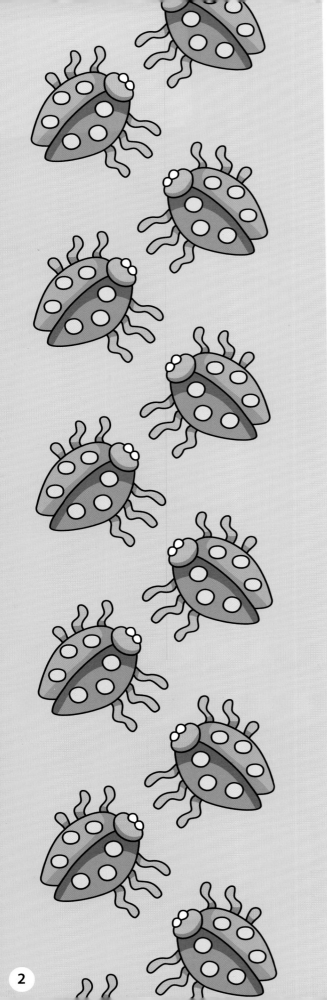

Produced by:

Kooler Design Studio, Inc.
399 Taylor Blvd., Suite 104
Pleasant Hill, CA 94523
kds@koolerdesign.com

Published by:

LEISURE ARTS.
the art of everyday living

Copyright ©2007 by Leisure Arts, Inc.,
5701 Ranch Drive, Little Rock, AR 72223
www.leisurearts.com

Production Team:
- Creative Director: Donna Kooler
- Editor-In-Chief: Judy Swager
- Senior Graphic Designer: María Parrish
- Graphic Designer: Maura MacLean
- Photographer: Dianne Woods
- Photo Stylist: Basha Kooler
- Proofreader: Char Randolph

Contents

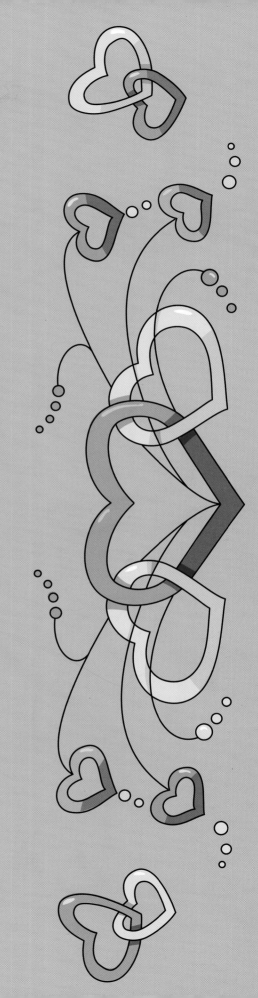

General Instructions

transfer basics

There are numerous ways to use the versatile designs in this book. The permanent iron-ons will usually transfer three times or more. You can iron them directly onto almost any fabric, article of clothing, or heavy paper, then embroider or color as you please. These designs are also fun to paint. Use traditional transferring methods to apply the designs to wood, tin, leather, or other surfaces. Customize the designs to fit your needs by enlarging and reducing them on a copy machine.

transferring on fabric and paper

Included in the book are small test transfers. Use them on a scrap of fabric or paper similar to your project to help you determine the best iron temperature and length of time needed to achieve a good transfer. The printed transfer is permanent once it is heat-set, so it is important to follow the steps below before transferring your design to clothing, fabric, or paper.

1. Before starting your project, be sure the test transfer and/or page number have been removed from the design area of your transfer.
2. If you are transferring a design to a fabric item that will be washed, first wash and dry the item without using fabric softener; press.
3. Preheat the iron for five minutes on appropriate setting for item being used. **Do not** use steam.
4. Because transfer ink may bleed through fabric, it's important to protect the ironing surface with a clean piece of scrap fabric or paper.
5. Place transfer **inked side down** on the **right side** of fabric or paper. For fabric projects, pin around outside of design to hold in place. Cover the design area with a piece of tissue paper. Place your hot iron on top of transfer; hold for 10-15 seconds (or time determined with your test pattern). **Do not** slide iron. Lift straight up and down and apply even pressure. For large transfers, pick up iron and move to another position until you've applied the entire design. Carefully lift one corner of transfer to see if design has been transferred to item. If not, place iron on transfer for a few more seconds.

alternative transferring method

Transfers may not show up on dark fabrics, but you can easily transfer the designs using white or light-colored dressmaker's tracing paper.

1. Pull fabric taut over a piece of cardboard covered with plastic to provide a smooth area for transferring and, later, for protecting your work surface from any paint that may soak through the fabric.
2. Trace the design onto transparent tracing paper. Flip design for the correct orientation and place on fabric in desired position.
3. Slip the dressmaker's tracing paper, coated side down, between the traced design and the fabric; tape or pin design and fabric to hold in place. Use a tracing wheel, stylus, or dull pencil to draw over design lines.

transferring on wood and other surfaces

1. Prepare your surface for painting as needed.
2. Apply an overall background color to the surface. Keep the surface as smooth and even as possible by painting with a large brush and applying several light coats rather than a single heavy one. Always let the paint dry between coats.
3. Trace the design onto transparent tracing paper. Flip the tracing over for correct orientation and tape to the surface in desired position. Slip a piece of transfer or graphite paper underneath the tracing with colored side down. Use gray paper for projects with light backgrounds and white paper for projects with dark backgrounds.
4. Trace over the design using a pencil, inkless pen, or small end of a stylus.

gathering embroidery supplies

Embroidery supplies are easy to find at your local craft, fabric, or needlework store. Needle, thread, fabric, scissors, and a hoop are all you'll need for most projects, although if you are working with stretchable fabrics you should also have some fabric stabilizer.

Needle: Any needle that you can easily thread and pass smoothly through the fabric will be fine. If your fabric has an open weave, it will accommodate a larger needle and heavier thread. For finer weaves, a sharp, slender needle will be the best choice.

Thread: Six-strand embroidery floss and perle cotton are the most common threads used for embroidery, however, when you have some experience, you may want to try rayon, metallics, ribbon, or anything else you can thread through a needle. We recommend using 3 strands of floss from the 6-strand skein. Use 2 strands for a more delicate look and finer fabrics or 4 strands for heavier coverage. Cut floss into 18" lengths. Floss this length does not fray or tangle as easily as longer lengths. Floss purchased from your local retailer is reliably colorfast, but if you're using floss from grandma's stash or a garage sale, it's a good idea to set the floss color before stitching. This is especially important when working with dark floss on light fabric. To set the color, soak floss in a mixture of 1 tablespoon vinegar and 8 ounces of water, then allow to air dry.

Fabric: If you are new to embroidery, we recommend stitching on 100% cotton or light linen. Once you feel comfortable with these, you'll be ready to branch out to other fabrics. Keep in mind that stiff and heavy fabrics are harder to embroider, since the needle won't slip through them as easily. Cotton knits and stretchable terries are also more difficult to stitch and require a stabilizing fabric to keep them from stretching.

Scissors: Embroidery scissors with short blades and narrow pointed tips are best. They will give you a sharp edge when cutting your thread (really helpful when threading the needle!), and you can use the pointed tips for pulling out any unwanted stitches.

Embroidery Hoop: This tool is optional but is very useful in keeping the stitching and fabric smooth. Choose a hoop that best fits the size of the design you are embroidering, although for larger designs just move the hoop around the fabric.

Stabilizer: When stitching on stretchy fabrics such as T-shirts or cotton knits, place a stabilizer on the back of the fabric to give the embroidery a layer of support and keep the fabric from stretching. Some stabilizers tear away when the embroidery is complete while others provide a permanent backing. Ask your retailer for advice on which stabilizing product is best to use with your particular fabric.

let's embroider

Now that your design is transferred to the fabric and you've gathered your materials, you're all set to embellish with beautiful embroidered accents. Because the iron-on transfer ink is permanent, be sure your stitches cover all transfer lines. On the following page you'll find illustrations and instructions for some of the most popular embroidery stitches. Suggested uses for stitches include: Backstitches, Running Stitches, or Stem Stitches for lettering, outlining, and flower stems; Satin Stitches when a solid look is desired for berries, small leaves, and flower petals; French Knots for flower centers, small berries, and eyes; Lazy Daisy Stitches for small flower petals and leaves; Straight Stitches to add detail lines to small areas. Refer to the project gallery on pages 43-48 for ideas showing where to use the various stitches.

backstitch

Come up at 1, go down at 2, and come up at 3 . Continue working as shown. Length of stitches may be varied as desired.

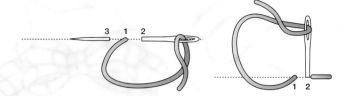

running stitch

The running stitch consists of a series of straight stitches with the stitch length equal to the space between stitches.

french knot

Come up at 1. Wrap thread twice around needle and insert needle at 2, holding end of thread with non-stitching fingers. Tighten knot; then pull needle through, holding floss until it must be released. For larger knot, use more strands; wrap only once.

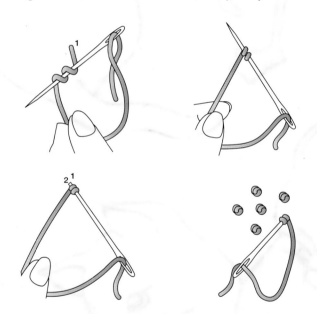

satin stitch

Come up at 1. Go down at 2, and come up at 3. Continue until area is filled.

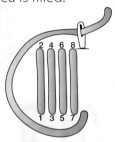

stem stitch

Come up at 1. Keeping thread below stitching line, go down at 2 and come up at 3. Go down at 4 and come up at 5.

lazy daisy stitch

Bring needle up at 1; take needle down again at 1 but not in the same hole to form a loop; bring needle up at 2. Keeping loop below point of needle, take needle down at 3 to anchor loop.

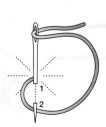

straight stitch

Bring needle up at 1 and take needle down at 2. Length of stitches may be varied as desired.

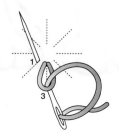

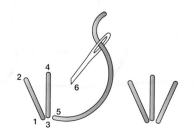

test pattern

8

test pattern

EX-LIBRIS

13

test pattern

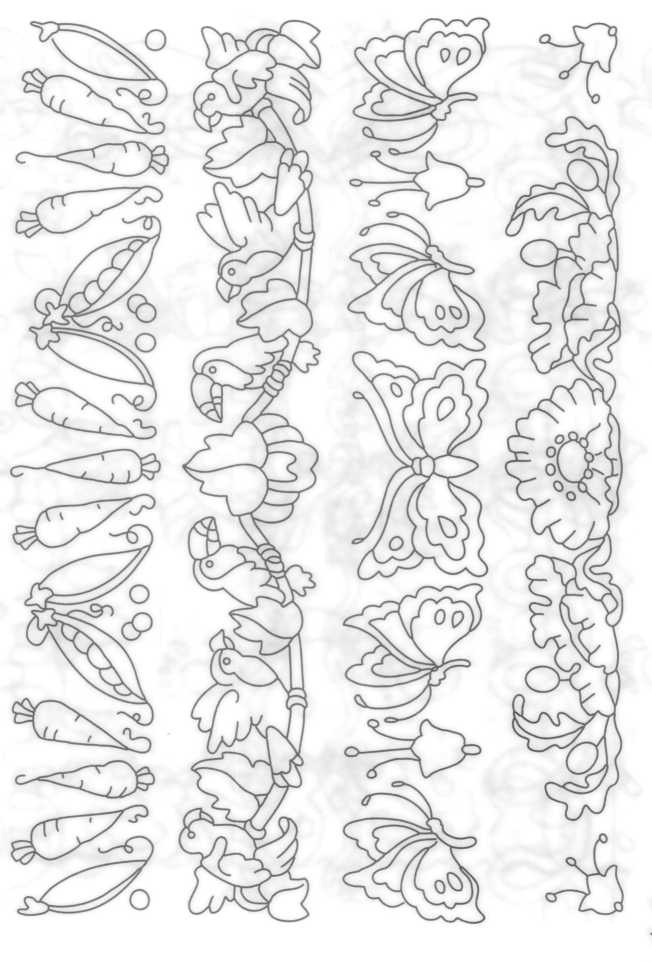

14
test pattern

test pattern

test pattern

test pattern

test pattern

test pattern

test pattern

BED 'N
BREAKFAST

WELCOME
FRIENDS

27
test pattern

test pattern

test pattern

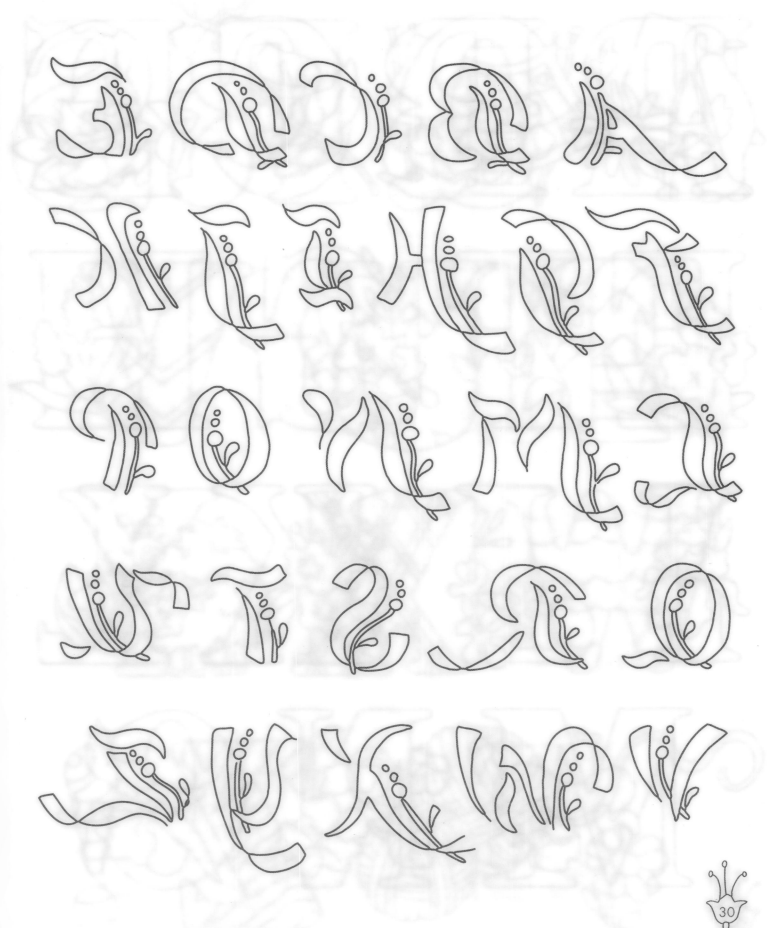

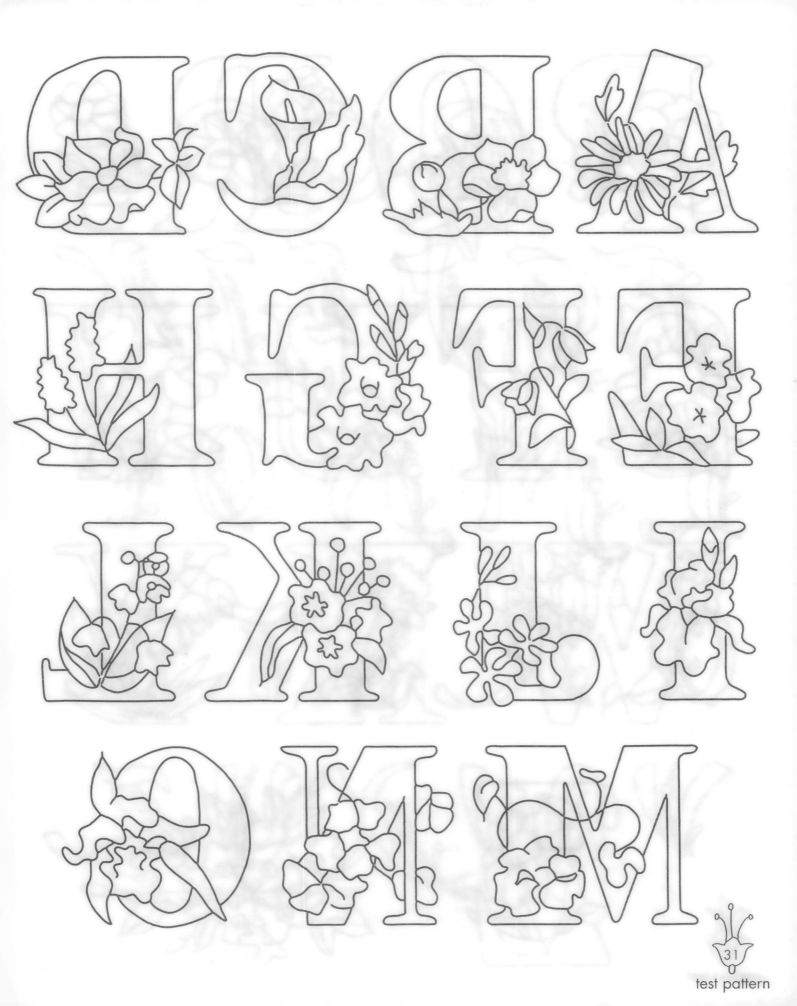

test pattern

test pattern

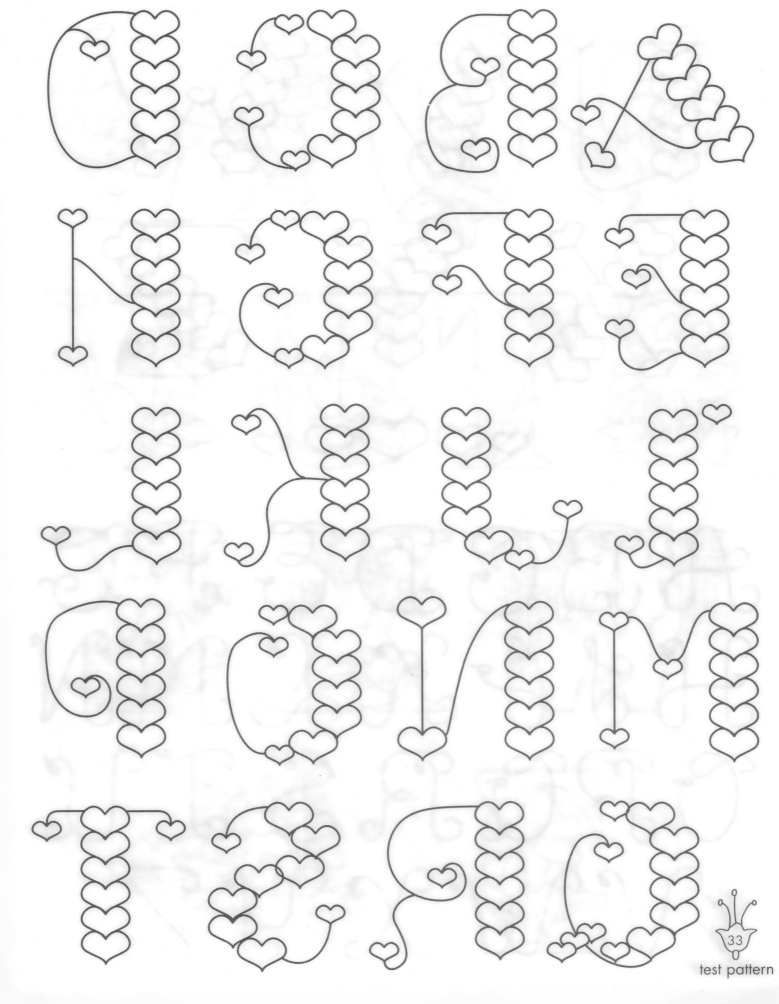

test pattern

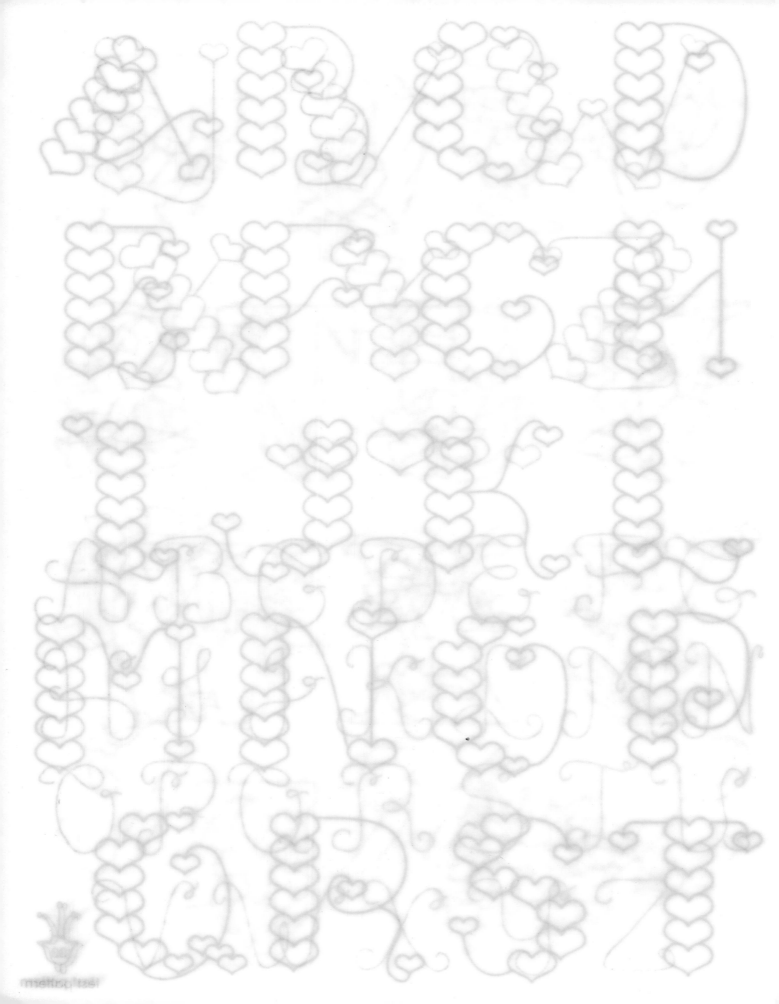

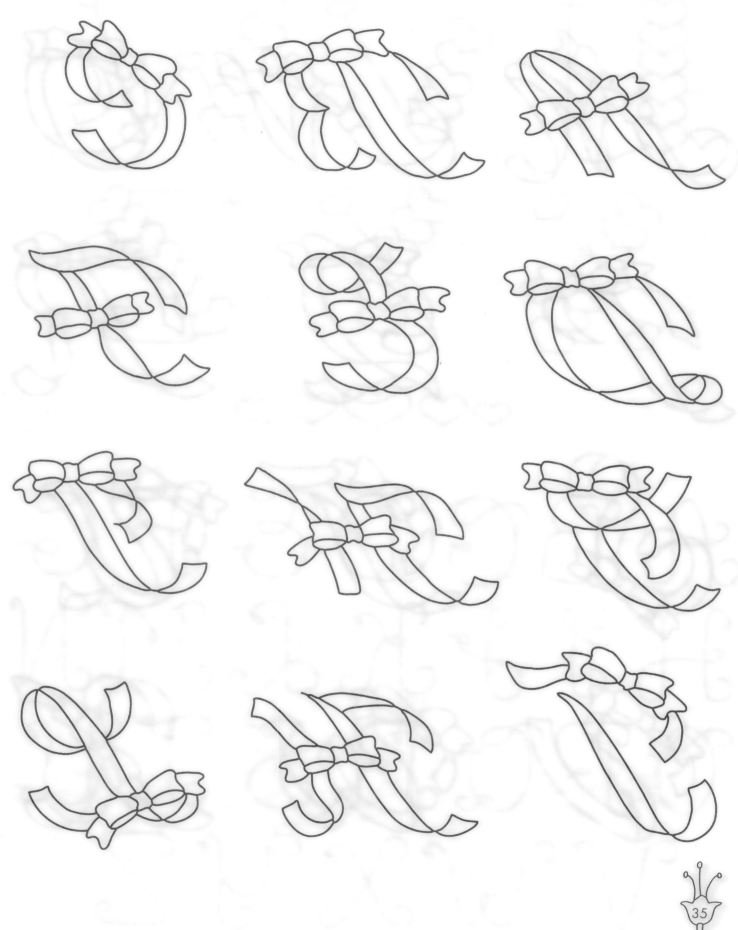

test pattern

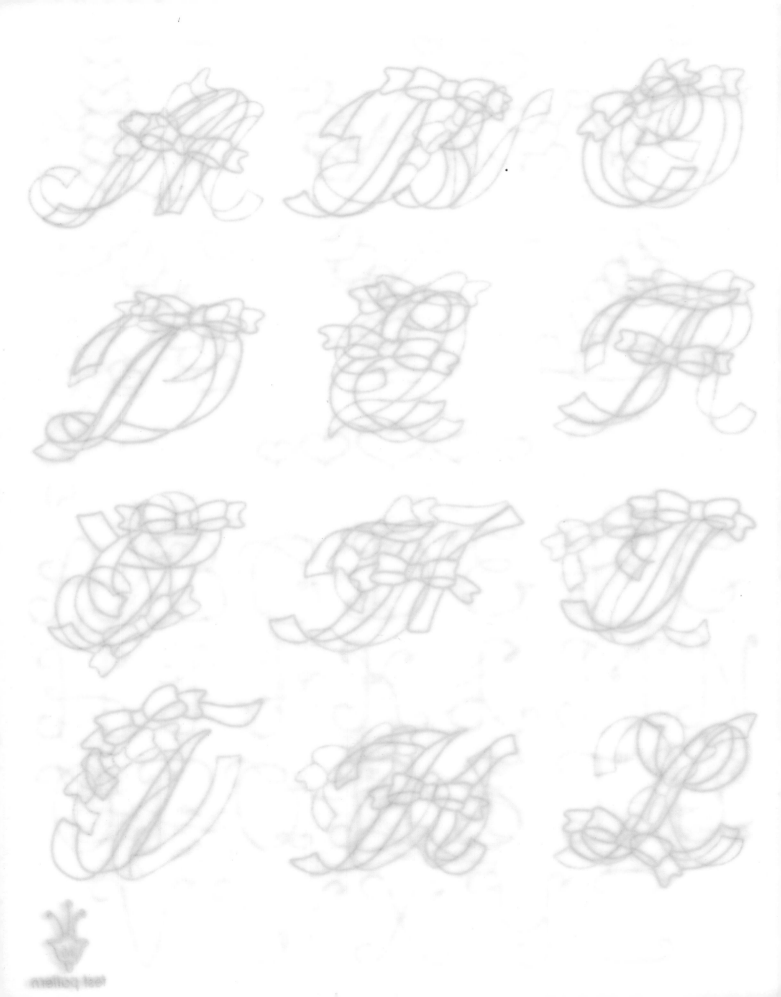

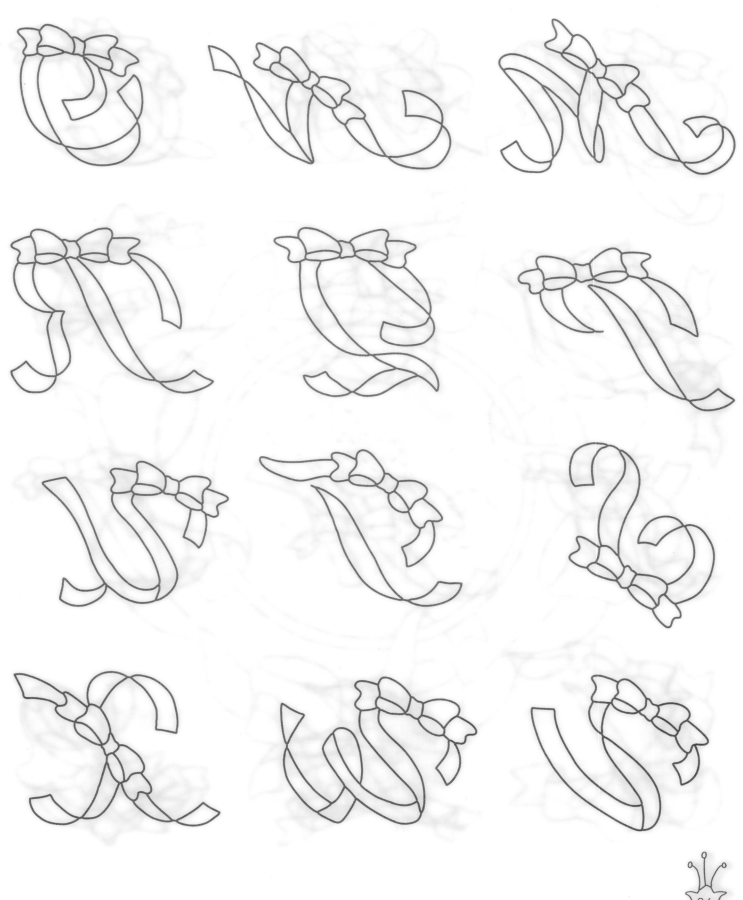

test pattern

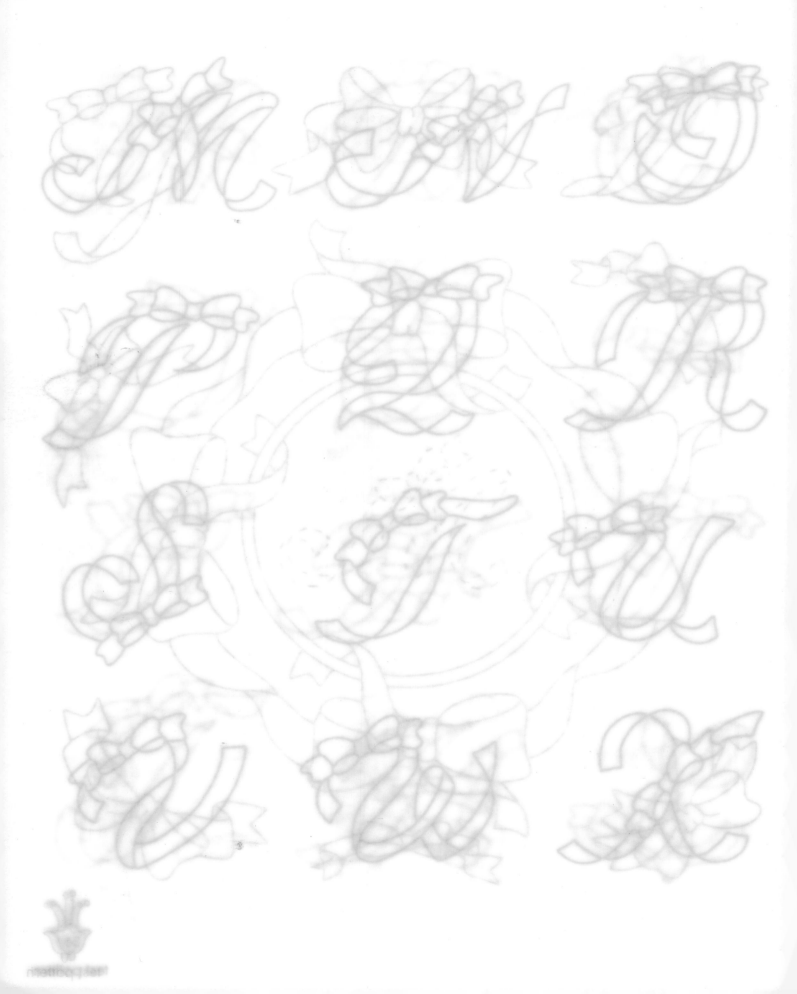

test pattern

test pattern

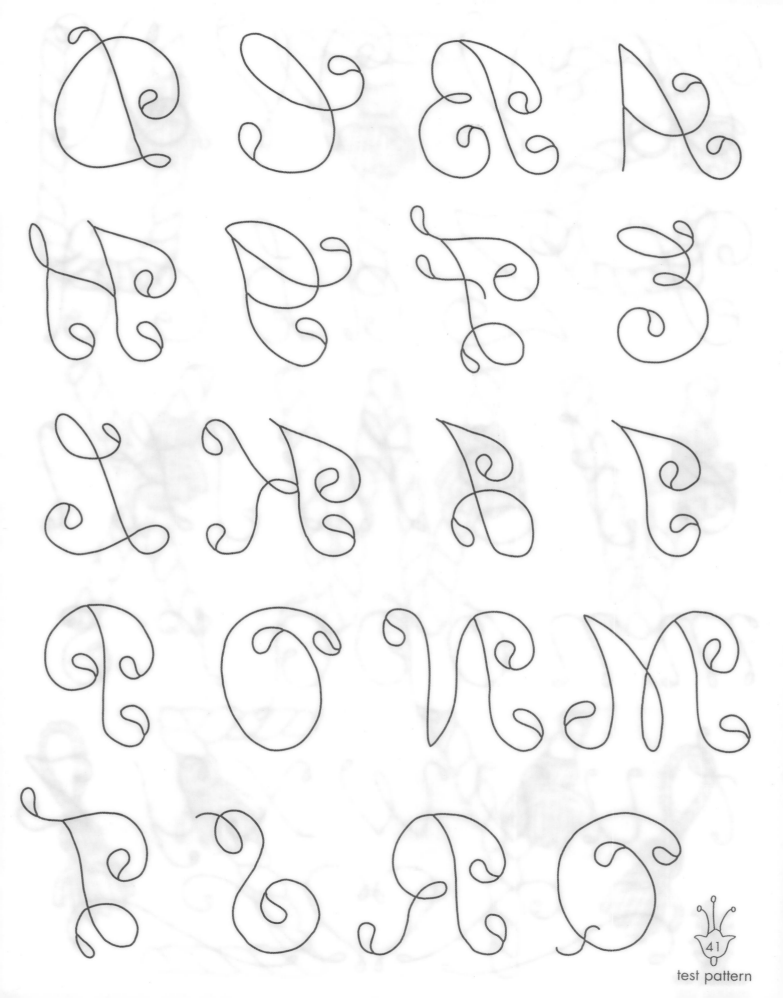

test pattern

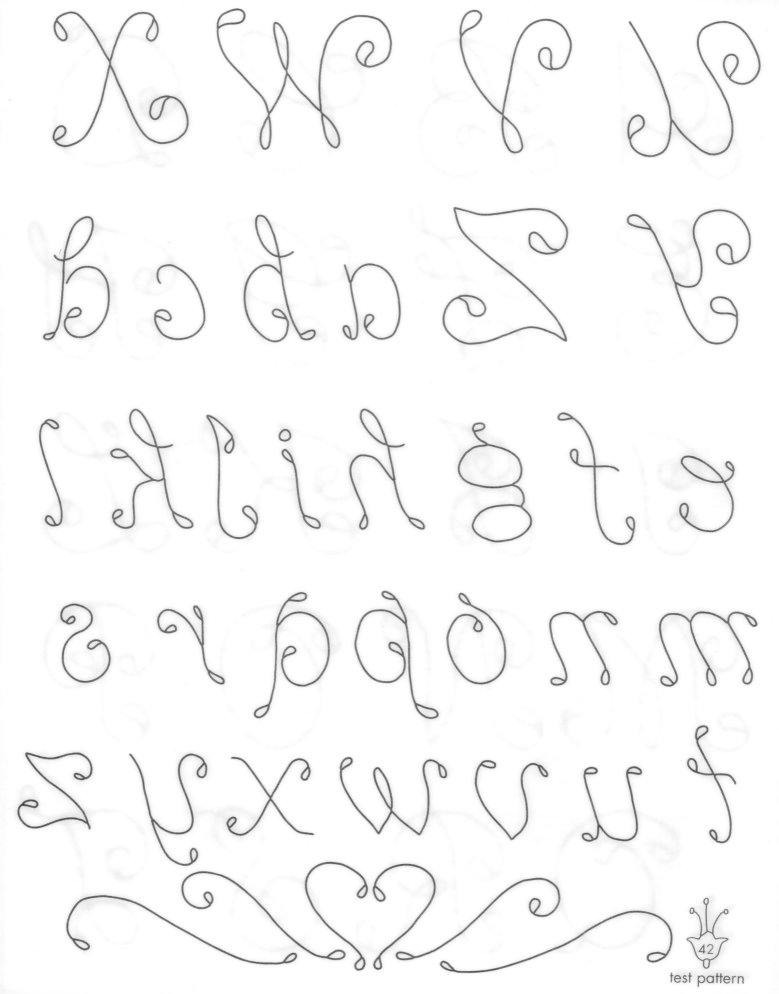

test pattern

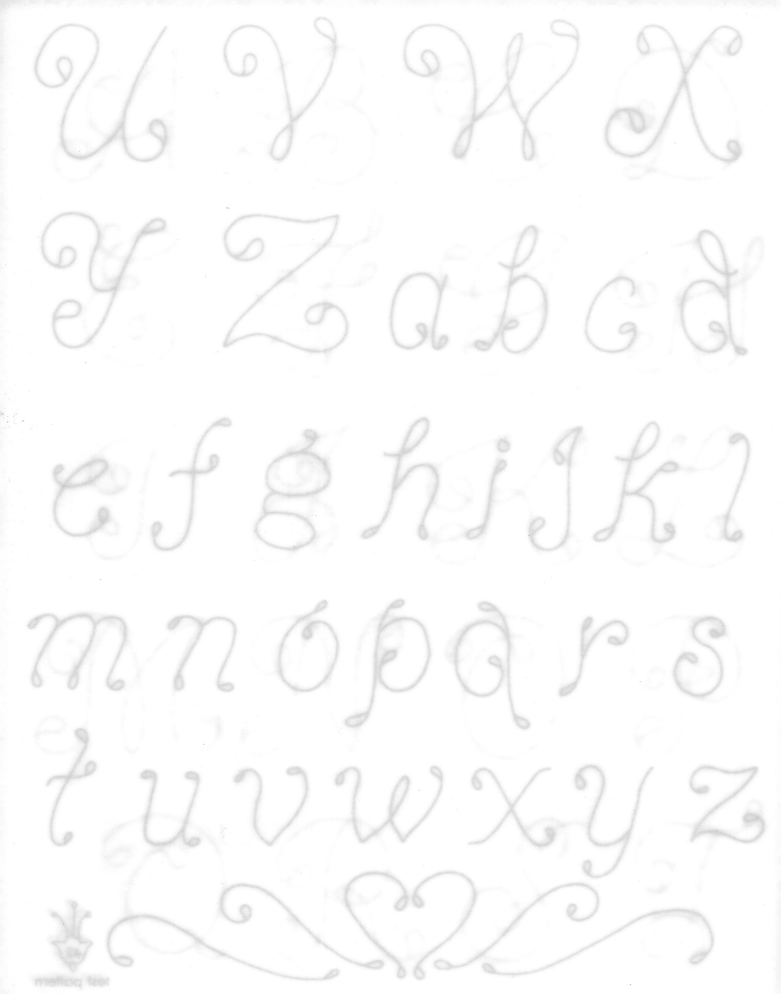

Gallery

Wow! This portion of the book contains many creative examples of what you can do with the 200+ iron-on transfer designs in this book. Mix and match to transform any wardrobe into designer originals by selecting from your favorite motifs, holidays, and hobbies; they are great on T-shirts, all types of denim, canvas bags, aprons, kids' clothing, table linens, handkerchiefs, and much more.